KAMOLOVA SAIDA ZUFAR QIZI

Manual For Reading Short Stories

Guidebook

© Kamolova Saida Zufar Qizi
Manual For Reading Short Stories
by: Kamolova Saida Zufar Qizi
Edition: July '2024
Publisher:
Taemeer Publications LLC (Michigan, USA / Hyderabad, India)

ISBN 978-93-5872-570-4

© **Kamolova Saida Zufar Qizi**

Book	:	Manual For Reading Short Stories
Author	:	Kamolova Saida Zufar Qizi
Publisher	:	Taemeer Publications
Year	:	'2024
Pages	:	118
Title Design	:	*Taemeer Web Design*

INTRODUCTION

This book consists of five different and entertaining short stories in English. The stories, which were written by different authors are for pre-intermediate learners, equivalent to B1-B2 on the Common European Framework of Reference (CEFR). Reading these stories give readers four opportunities:
- ✓ to improve English
- ✓ to spend time efficiently by reading
- ✓ to learn by heart various vocabulary in easy ways
- ✓ to boost reading skills through doing exercises and tests

Reading books is considered to be one of the best ways to enhance your English as well as to widen your world outlook.

Reading this book, you will not only enjoy discovering different worlds in English, but also you will learn different grammatical structure as well as words used regularly!

There are many useful activities in the book that help you read more effectively. For example, after each chapter or each story, there are four activities:
- ✓ Matching the words with synonyms
- ✓ True / false questions

- ✓ Multiple choice questions
- ✓ Writing a short review for each story

So, make a cup of coffee, sit comfortably and open the chapters. It's high time to make your imagination run wild and enter a magical English world!

GOOD LUCK!!!

Table of Contents

1. *The gift of the Magi*
2. *Sermons in stones at Bloomsbury. The new sculpture room at the British museum*
3. *The church*
4. *Persistence pays*
5. *Discussion on Dating*
   <u>Activities for each story</u>

- ➢ New vocabulary with their definition in english
- ➢ True/False question
- ➢ Matching
- ➢ Different questions
- ➢ Write a short review for each story
- ➢ Answers

Story-1
The gift of the Magi
(by O. Henry)
Chapter-1

One dollar and eighty-seven cents. That was all. And sixty cents of it was in pennies. Pennies saved one and two at a time by bulldozing the grocer and the vegetable man and the butcher until one's cheeks burned with the silent imputation of parsimony that such close dealing implied. Three times Della counted it. One dollar and eighty- seven cents. And the next day would be Christmas.

There was clearly nothing to do but flop down on the shabby little couch and howl. So Della did it. Which instigates the moral reflection that life is made up of sobs, sniffles, and smiles, with sniffles predominating.

While the mistress of the home is gradually subsiding from the first stage to the second, take a look at the home. A furnished flat at $8 per week. It did not exactly beggar description, but it certainly had that word on the lookout for the mendicancy squad.

In the vestibule below was a letter-box into which no letter would go, and an electric button from which no mortal finger could coax a ring. Also appertaining thereunto was a card bearing the name "Mr. James Dillingham Young."

The "Dillingham" had been flung to the breeze during a former period of prosperity when its possessor was being paid $30 per week. Now, when the income was shrunk to

$20, though, they were thinking seriously of contracting to a modest and unassuming D. But whenever Mr. James Dillingham Young came home and reached his flat above he was called "Jim" and greatly hugged by Mrs. James Dillingham Young, already introduced to you as Della. Which is all very good.

Della finished her cry and attended to her cheeks with the powder rag. She stood by the window and looked out dully at a gray cat walking a gray fence in a gray backyard. Tomorrow would be Christmas Day, and she had only $1.87 with which to buy Jim a present. She had been saving every penny she could for months, with this result. Twenty dollars a week doesn't go far. Expenses had been greater than she had calculated. They always are. Only $1.87 to buy a present for Jim. Her Jim. Many a happy hour she had spent planning for something nice for him. Something fine and rare and sterling-- something just a little bit near to being worthy of the honor of being owned by Jim.

There was a pier-glass between the windows of the room. Perhaps you have seen a pier-glass in an $8 flat. A very thin and very agile person may, by observing his reflection in a rapid sequence of longitudinal strips, obtain a fairly accurate conception of his looks. Della, being slender, had mastered the art.

Suddenly she whirled from the window and stood before the glass. her eyes were shining brilliantly, but her face had lost its color within twenty seconds. Rapidly she pulled down her hair and let it fall to its full length.

Now, there were two possessions of the James Dillingham Youngs in which they both took a mighty pride. One was Jim's gold watch that had been his father's and his grandfather's. The other was Della's hair. Had the queen of Sheba lived in the flat across the airshaft, Della would have let her hair hang out the window someday to dry just

to depreciate Her Majesty's jewels and gifts. Had King Solomon been the janitor, with all his treasures piled up in the basement, Jim would have pulled out his watch every time he passed, just to see him pluck at his beard from envy.

So now Della's beautiful hair fell about her rippling and shining like a cascade of brown waters. It reached below her knee and made itself almost a garment for her. And then she did it up again nervously and quickly. Once she faltered for a minute and stood still while a tear or two splashed on the worn red carpet.

On went her old brown jacket; on went her old brown hat. With a whirl of skirts and with the brilliant sparkle still in her eyes, she fluttered out the door and down the stairs to the street. Where she stopped the sign read: "Mne. Sofronie. Hair Goods of All Kinds." One flight up Della ran, and collected herself, panting. Madame, large, too white, chilly, hardly looked the "Sofronie."

"Will you buy my hair?" asked Della.

"I buy hair," said Madame. "Take yer hat off and let's have a sight at the looks of it." Down rippled the brown cascade.

"Twenty dollars," said Madame, lifting the mass with a practised hand. "Give it to me quick," said Della.

Oh, and the next two hours tripped by on rosy wings. Forget the hashed metaphor. She was ransacking the stores for Jim's present.

She found it at last. It surely had been made for Jim and no one else. There was no other like it in any of the stores, and she had turned all of them inside out. It was a platinum fob chain simple and chaste in design, properly proclaiming its value by substance alone and not by meretricious ornamentation--as all good things should do. It was even worthy of The Watch. As soon as she saw it she knew that it must be Jim's. It was like him. Quietness and value--the description applied to both. Twenty-one dollars they took from her for it, and she hurried home with the 87 cents. With that chain on his watch Jim might be properly anxious about the time in any company. Grand as the watch was, he sometimes looked at it on the sly on account of the old leather strap that he used in place.

Vocabulary study

•**Imputation-***noun-* a statement which you say, often unfairly, that somebody is responsible for something or has a particular quality. [e.g. He denied the imputation.]

•**Parsimony-** *noun-* the fact of being extremely unwilling to spend money. [synonym- meanness]

•**Predominate-** *verb-* to be greater in amount or number than something/somebody else in a place, group, etc. [e.g. A young girl predominated the whole audience.]

•**Mistress-** *noun-* a man's mistress is a woman that he is having a regular sexual relationship with and who is not his wife. [e.g. The fact that he had a mistress was a lie, he was loyal to his wife.]

•**Longitudinal-** *adjective-* going downwards rather than across. [e.g. The plant's stem is marked with thin, green, longitudinal stripes.]

•**Cascade-** *noun* – a small waterfall, especially one of several falling down a steep slope with rocks. [e.g. a cascade of rainwater.]

•**Faltered-** *adjective-* becoming weaker or less effective.

- **Platinum-** *noun-* a chemical element,a silver-grey precious metal, used in making expensive jewellery and in industry
- **Proclaim-** *verb-*to publicly and officially tell people about something important. [e.g. The day was proclaimed a public holiday.]
- **Ornamentation-** *noun-*the use of objects, designs, etc. to decorate something. [e.g. The architect was instructed to keep ornamentation to a minimum

A. MATCH THE WORDS WITH THEIR DEFINITIONS

1. imputation	a-white gold
2. parsimony	b-decoration
3. mistress	c-declare
4. predominate	d-stinginess
5. cascade	e-accusing someone unfairly
6. longitudinal	f-fall
7. faltered	g-hesitant
8. platinum	h-be in the majority
9. proclaim	i-moving downwards
10. ornamentation	j- girlfriend

1.
2.
3.
4.
5.
6.
7.
8.
9.
10.

B. For each question, choose TRUE or FALSE options if the word in italics has been used correctly

1. Della counted the pennies saved more than three times.
   TRUE__ FALSE__
2. There was clearly One dollar and eighty-seven cents to do but flop down on the shabby little

couch and howl.
TRUE__ FALSE__
3. The "Dillingham" had been flung to the breeze during a former period of prosperity when its possessor was being paid $30 per week.
TRUE__ FALSE__
4. there were two possessions of the James Dillingham Youngs in which they both took a mighty pride.
TRUE__ FALSE__
5. Possession was Jim's brilliant watch that had been his father's and his grandfather's.
TRUE_ FALSE__
6. Della's beautiful hair fell about her rippling and shining like a cascade of brown waters. It reached below her knee and made itself almost a garment for her.
TRUE__ FALSE__
7. Madame bought Della's long hair and paid her thirty dollars.
TRUE__ FALSE__
8. …As soon as she saw THE WATCH she knew that it must be Jim's.
TRUE_ FALSE_

C. Read the story again and circle the most appropriate answer to the question.
1. What was there to do but flop down on the shabby little couch and howl?
a) Nearly nothing
b) One dollar and eighty-seven cents.

c) Pennies only
2. How much did A furnished flat cost per week?
a) Twenty dollars
b) Eight dollars
c) Seven dollars
3. When was the possessor being paid $30 per week?.
a) When income was shrunk to 210 dollars
b) When income was shrunk to 11 dollars
c) When income was shrunk to 20 dollars
4. What was Della's hair look like?
a) like a cascade of brown waters
b) like brown waters.
c) like a cascade

D. Write a short review for the story

_____
_____
_____
_____
_____
_____
_____
_____

Chapter-2

When Della reached home her, intoxication gave way a little to prudence and reason. She got out her curling irons and lighted the gas and went to work repairing the ravages made by generosity added to love. Which is always a tremendous task, dear friends--a mammoth task.

Within forty minutes her head was covered with tiny, close-lying curls that made her look wonderfully like a truant schoolboy. She looked at her reflection in the mirror long, carefully, and critically.

"If Jim doesn't kill me," she said to herself, "before he takes a second look at me, he'll say I look like a Coney Island chorus girl. But what could I do--oh! what could I do with a dollar and eighty- seven cents?"

At 7 o'clock the coffee was made and the frying-pan was on the back of the stove hot and ready to cook the chops.

Jim was never late. Della doubled the fob chain in her hand and sat on the corner of the table near the door that he always entered. Then she heard his step on the stair away down on the first flight, and she turned white for just a moment. She had a habit for saying little silent prayer about the simplest everyday things, and now she whispered: "Please God, make him think I am still pretty."

The door opened and Jim stepped in and

closed it. He looked thin and very serious. Poor fellow, he was only twenty-two--and to be burdened with a family! He needed a new overcoat and he was without gloves.

Jim stopped inside the door, as immovable as a setter at the scent of quail. His eyes were fixed upon Della, and there was an expression in them that she could not read, and it terrified her. It was not anger, nor surprise, nor disapproval, nor horror, nor any of the sentiments that she had been prepared for. He simply stared at her fixedly with that peculiar expression on his face.

Della wriggled off the table and went for him.

"Jim, darling," she cried, "don't look at me that way. I had my hair cut off and sold because I couldn't have lived through Christmas without giving you a present. It'll grow out again--you won't mind, will you? I just had to do it. My hair grows awfully fast. Say

`Merry Christmas!' Jim, and let's be happy. You don't know what a nice-- what a beautiful, nice gift I've got for you."

"You've cut off your hair?" asked Jim, laboriously, as if he had not arrived at that patent fact yet even after the hardest mental labor. "Cut it off and sold it," said Della. "Don't you like me just as well, anyhow? I'm me without my hair, ain't I?"

Jim looked about the room curiously.

"You say your hair is gone?" he said, with an air almost of idiocy.

"You needn't look for it," said Della. "It's sold, I tell you--sold and gone, too. It's Christmas Eve, boy. Be good to me, for it went for you. Maybe the hairs of my head were numbered," she went on with sudden serious sweetness, "but nobody could ever count my love for you. Shall I put the chops on, Jim?"

Out of his trance Jim seemed quickly to wake. He enfolded his Della. For ten seconds let us regard with discreet scrutiny some inconsequential object in the other direction.

Eight dollars a week or a million a year-- what is the difference? A mathematician or a wit would give you the wrong answer. The magi brought valuable gifts, but that was not among them. This dark assertion will be illuminated later on.

Jim drew a package from his overcoat pocket and threw it upon the table.

"Don't make any mistake, Dell," he said, "about me. I don't think there's anything in the way of a haircut or a shave or a shampoo that could make me like my girl any less. But if you'll unwrap that package you may see why you had me going a while at first."

White fingers and nimble tore at the string and paper. And then an ecstatic scream of joy; and then, alas! a quick feminine change to hysterical tears and wails, necessitating the immediate employment of all the comforting powers of the lord of the flat.

For there lay The Combs--the set of combs, side and back, that Della had worshipped long in a Broadway window. Beautiful combs, pure tortoise shell, with jewelled rims-- just the shade to wear in the beautiful vanished hair. They were expensive combs, she knew, and her heart had simply craved and yearned over them without the least hope of possession. And now, they were hers, but the tresses that should have adorned the coveted adornments were gone.

But she hugged them to her bosom, and at length she was able to look up with dim eyes and a smile and say: "My hair grows so fast, Jim!"

And them Della leaped up like a little singed cat and cried, "Oh, oh!"

Jim had not yet seen his beautiful present. She held it out to him eagerly upon her open palm. The dull precious metal seemed to flash with a reflection of her bright and ardent spirit.

"Isn't it a dandy, Jim? I hunted all over town to find it. You'll have to look at the time a hundred times a day now. Give me your watch. I want to see how it looks on it."

Instead of obeying, Jim tumbled down on the couch and put his hands under the back of his head and smiled.

"Dell," said he, "let's put our Christmas

presents away and keep them a while. They're too nice to use just at present. I sold the watch to get the money to buy your combs. And now suppose you put the chops on."

The magi, as you know, were wise men--wonderfully wise men--who brought gifts to the Babe in the manger. They invented the art of giving Christmas presents. Being wise, their gifts were no doubt wise ones, possibly bearing the privilege of exchange in case of duplication. And here I have lamely related to you the uneventful chronicle of two foolish children in a flat who most unwisely sacrificed for each other the greatest treasures of their house. But in a last word to the wise of these days let it be said that of all who give gifts these two were the wisest. O all who give and receive gifts, such as they are wisest. Everywhere they are wisest. They are the magi.

Vocabulary study

- **Intoxication-***noun*- the statement of being under the influence of alcohol or drugs
- **Prudence-** *noun*- a sensible and careful attitude when you make judgements and decisions; behaviour that avoids unnecessary risks
- **Truant-** *noun*- a child who stays away from school without permission
- **To be burdened with-***verb*- to be carrying something heavy.[e.g. She got off the bus ,

burdened with two heavy suitcases.
- **Scrutiny-noun-**careful and complete examination
- **Inconsequential-adjective-** not important or considering [e.g. The speech was full of inconsequential details.]
- **Necessitate-** *verb-* to make something important
- **Adorn-** *verb-* to make something or somebody look more attractive by decorating it or them with something
- **Ardent-** adjective- very enthusiastic and showing strong feelings about something or about somebody
- **Sacrifice-** *verb-* to give up something that is important or valuable to you in order to get or do something that seems more important for yourself or for another person

A. MATCH THE WORDS WITH THEIR SYNONYMS

Intoxication	trivial
Prudence	surrender
Truant	Feeling after alcohol
To be burdened with	wisdom
Scrutiny	Make smth important
Inconsequential	runaway

Necessitate	inspection
Adorn	passionate
Ardent	To weigh down
).Sacrifice	decorate

1.   *6.*
2.   *7.*
3.   *8.*
4.   *9.*
5.   *10.*

B. *For each question, choose TRUE or FALSE options if the word in italics has been used correctly*

1. She got out her curling irons and lighted the gas and went to work repairing the ravages made by generosity added to love.
   TRUE__ FALSE__
2. Within forty minutes her head was covered with tiny, close-lying curls that made her look wonderfully like a cute girl.
   TRUE__ FALSE__
3. Jim was always late.
   TRUE__ FALSE__
4. Della had her hair cut off and sold because she couldn't have lived through Christmas without giving him a present.
   TRUE__ FALSE__
5. The magi, as you know, were wise men-- wonderfully wise men--who brought gifts to the

Babe in the manger.
TRUE__ FALSE__
6. All who give and receive gifts, such as they are wisest.
TRUE__ FALSE__
7. They were not expensive combs, she knew, and her heart had simply craved and yearned over them with the hope of possession.
TRUE___FALSE__
8. Della leaped up like a little singed mouse and cried.
TRUE__ FALSE__

C. Read the story again and circle the most appropriate answer to the question.
1. What did intoxication give Della?
a) gave way a little to prudence and reason
b) gave way to earn money for a present
c) gave way to make a present.
2. Within forty minutes her head was covered with tiny, close-lying curls that made her look wonderfully like……………..
a) A cute child
b) a truant schoolboy
c) a princess
3. When did she turn white?
a) When she realized that she lost her last money
b) When she made presents
c) When she heard his step on the stair away down on the first flight
4. Why had Della my hair cut off and sold?

a) Because she need money
b) Because she was ill
c) Because she couldn't have lived through Christmas without giving a present.
5. What do you think what influenced them to do their best to buy presents?
a) Love between them
b) Hatred
c) Christmas

D. Write a short review for the story

_____
_____
_____
_____
_____
_____
_____
_____
_____

Story-2
SERMONS IN STONES AT BLOOMSBURY
THE NEW SCULPTURE ROOM AT THE BRITISH MUSEUM
(by Oscar Wilde)

Through the exertions of Sir Charles Newton, to whom every student of classic art should be grateful, some of the wonderful treasures so long immured in the grimy vaults of the British Museum have at last been brought to light, and the new Sculpture Room now opened to the public will amply repay the trouble of a visit, even from those to whom art is a stumbling-block and a rock of offence.

For setting aside the mere beauty of form, outline and mass, the grace and loveliness of design and the delicacy of technical treatment, here we have shown to us what the Greeks and Romans thought about death; and the philosopher, the preacher, the practical man of the world, and even the Philistine himself, cannot fail to be touched by these "sermons in stones," with their deep significance, their fertile suggestion, their plain humanity. Common tombstones they are, most of them, the work not of famous artists but of simple handicraftsmen, only they were wrought in days when every handicraft was an art.

The finest specimens, from the purely artistic point of view, are undoubtedly the two stelai found at Athens. They are both the tombstones of young Greek athletes. In one the athlete is represented handing his strigil to his slave, in the other the athlete stands alone, strigil in hand. They do not belong to the greatest period of Greek art, they have not the grand style of the Phidian age, but they are beautiful for all that, and it is impossible not to be fascinated by their exquisite grace and by the treatment which is so simple in its means, so subtle in its effect. All the tombstones, however, are full of interest.

Here is one of two ladies of Smyrna who were so remarkable in their day that the city voted them honorary crowns; here is a Greek doctor examining a little boy who is suffering from indigestion; here is the memorial of Xanthippus who, probably, was a martyr to gout, as he is holding in his hand the model of a foot, intended, no doubt, as a votive offering to some god.

A lovely stele from Rhodes gives us a family group. The husband is on horseback and is bidding farewell to his wife, who seems as if she would follow him but is being held back by a little child. The pathos of parting from those we love is the central motive of Greek funeral art. It is repeated in every possible form, and each mute marble stone seems to murmur [Greek text].

Roman art is different. It introduces vigorous and realistic portraiture and deals with pure family life far more frequently than Greek art does. They are very ugly, those stern-looking Roman men and women whose portraits are exhibited on their tombs, but they seem to have been loved and respected by their children and their servants.

Here is the monument of Aphrodisius and Atilia, a Roman gentleman and his wife, who died in Britain many centuries ago, and whose tombstone was found in the Thames; and close by it stands a stele from Rome with the busts of an old married couple who are certainly marvellously ill- favoured. The contrast between the abstract Greek treatment of the idea of death and the Roman concrete realization of the individuals who have died is extremely curious.

Besides the tombstones, the new Sculpture Room contains some most fascinating examples of Roman decorative art under the Emperors. The most wonderful of all, and this alone is worth a trip to Bloomsbury, is a bas-relief representing a marriage scene, Juno Pronuba is joining the hands of a handsome young noble and a very stately lady. There is all the grace of Perugino in this marble, all the grace of Raphael even. The date of it is uncertain, but the particular cut of the bridegroom's beard seems to point to the time of the Emperor Hadrian. It is clearly the work of Greek artists and is one of the most beautiful bas-reliefs in the whole Museum. There is something in it which reminds one of the music and the sweetness of Propertian verse. Then we have delightful friezes of children. One representing children playing on musical instruments might have suggested much of the plastic art of Florence. Indeed, as we view these marbles it is not difficult to see whence the Renaissance sprang and to what we owe the various forms of Renaissance art. The frieze of the Muses, each of whom wears in her hair a feather plucked from the wings of the vanquished sirens, is extremely fine; there is a lovely little bas-relief of two cupids racing in chariots; and the frieze of recumbent Amazons has some splendid qualities of design. A frieze of children playing with the armour of the god Mars should also be mentioned. It is full of fancy and delicate humour.

  We hope that some more of the hidden treasures will shortly be catalogued and shown. In the vaults at present there is a very remarkable bas-relief of the marriage of Cupid and Psyche, and another representing the professional mourners weeping over the body of the dead. The fine cast of the Lion of Chaeronea should also be brought up, and so should the stele with the marvellous portrait of the Roman slave. Economy is an excellent public virtue, but the parsimony that allows valuable works of art to remain in the grim and gloom of a damp cellar is little short of a detestable public.

Vocabulary study

- **Exertion -*noun*-** physical or mental effort; the act of making an effort [e.g. she was hot and breathless from the exertion of cycling uphill.]
- **Delicacy- *noun*-** the fact of being or appearing to be; easy to damage or break.
- **Indigestion- *noun*-** pain caused by difficulty in digesting food. [Rich food always gives me indigestion.]
- **Memorial- adjective-** created or done in order to remember somebody who is rest in peace.
- **Stern-looking-adjective-** serious and showing that you do not approve of somebody or something; expecting somebody to obey you.
- **Vanquished-adjective-** completely defeated in a competition, war, etc.
- **Recumbent-adjective-**(of a person's body or position) lying down
- **Splendid-adjective-** very impressive, very beautiful [e.g. He made a lot of money and had a splendid house built.]
- **Marvellous-adjective-** extremely good, wonderful. [e.g. the weather was marvellous.]
- **Detestable-adjective-**that deserves to be hated. [e.g. it is detestable.]

A. MATCH THE WORDS WITH THEIR

SYNONYMS

Exertion	loathsome
Delicacy	remembrance
Indigestion	Severe-looking
Memorial	conquered
Stern-looking	effort
Vanquished	lying
Recumbent	sensibility
splendid	great
marvellous	magnificen
.Detestable	Dyspepsia

1.   6.
2.   7.
3.   8.
4.   9.
5.   10.

B. *For each question, choose TRUE or FALSE options if the word in italics has been used correctly*

1. For setting aside the mere beauty of form, outline and mass, the grace and loveliness of design and the delicacy of technical treatment, here we have shown to us what the Greeks and Romans thought about death.
   TRUE__ FALSE__

2. Philosopher, the preacher, the practical man of the world, and even the Philistine himself, can fail to be touched by these "sermons in stones," with their deep significance, their fertile suggestion, their plain humanity.
   TRUE__ FALSE__
3. Common tombstones they are, most of them, the work not of famous artists but of simple handicraftsmen.
   TRUE____ FALSE__
4. Economy is an excellent public virtue, but the parsimony that allows valuable works of art to remain in the grim and gloom of a damp cellar is enormous part of a detestable public vice.
   TRUE___ FALSE__
5. There is something in it which reminds one of the music and the sweetness of Propertian verse.
   TRUE__ FALSE__
6. The most popular of all, and this alone is worth a trip to Bloomsbury, is a bas-relief representing a happiness scene, Juno Pronuba is joining the hands of a handsome young noble and a very stately lady.
   TRUE_ FALSE__
7. Roman art is different. It introduces vigorous and realistic portraiture and deals with pure family life far more frequently than Greek art does.
   TRUE_ FALSE__

C. Read the story again and circle the most appropriate answer to the question.

1. What is the central motive of Greek funeral art?
a) The pathos of parting from those we love
b) Their tradition
c) Their culture
2. What are undoubtedly the two stelai found?
a) The finest specimens, from the purely artistic point of view
b) The finest specimen
c) the purely artistic point of view
3. Give your definition for one of two ladies of Smyrna who were soremarkable in their day.
a) The most artistic work
b) the city voted them honorary crowns
c) that the city did not vote them honorary crowns

4. What does a lovely stele from Rhodes give us ?
a) A membership
b) A lovely couple
c) a family group

D. Write a short review for the story

_____
_____
_____
_____

Story-3
The Church
Chapter-1

The bus driver kept looking at Amber. He was staring at her using his rear-view mirror. She noticed that he had been doing it for a while. It was really starting to bother her.

Amber looked around at the empty seats on the bus. It was a large city bus. She was the last passenger on it. The city was asleep. It was almost two o'clock in the morning.

He keeps looking at me, Amber thought. I guess he thinks I'm very pretty.

But, he looks like a hairy caveman.

She tried to ignore him. She gazed out of her window into the darkness. They passed by dark buildings. Every building had its lights off. And, there were almost no other cars on the road…

Suddenly, she realized, I don't know which road we are on! This is not the street we should be on.

Alarmed, Amber turned her head and saw the bus driver. He was driving and smiling at nothing.

What is this guy doing??

She got out of her seat, holding her small purse. The bus ride had been very smooth, but when she started walking toward the front, one of the bus's wheels hit a hole in the road. Amber fell forward. She reached out her arm. She grabbed a seat back and caught herself from falling.

The bus driver laughed.

He drove into that pothole on purpose!

"Sit down, little lady!" the driver said. He had to take deep breaths after each sentence. He had some breathing problem. "We're on a rocky road now!"

"Excuse me, but which road are we on?" she asked. "Are you lost?"

"What do you mean? I never get lost!" He took a deep breath and laughed with his mouth opened wide. He was missing several teeth. He scratched at his beard and coughed. "I told you to sit down. It isn't safe to stand up while the bus is moving. We don't want you to hurt your pretty head. It might mess up your hairdo!"

Amber did not think the situation was funny. She had heard of things like this happening. But, she was not scared, not yet. She held her purse tighter and walked closer to the driver.

"Tell me where are you going? I do not recognize this road. This isn't the right way."

"It's right for me," the driver said mysteriously. Instead of looking at her in the mirror, he turned his head to stare at her. There were cookie crumbs in his beard. His eyes were red and bloodshot. Even from her distance away from him, Amber could smell him.

Did this guy take a shower this year? He really stinks!

Without warning, the bus driver reached out at her. Amber stepped backward, and he laughed again.

"I'm just messing with you," he said, breathing heavily. "Stop worrying, I am a professional. I know what I am doing."

Amber did not like this. She sat down and waited, wondering if she should make a phone call. He is acting weird, she thought, but maybe he really is lost. Sometimes, new drivers forget the roads. Maybe, he does not want to admit he is lost. He does not know where we are, but he feels embarrassed.

The driver began to slow down. Amber peeked out of the window. She did not see any street lights or stop signs. Why is he slowing down? Will he turn the bus around?

"Almost there," he said. He took a drink from a plastic bottle. Amber did not think it was water inside the bottle.

The bus pulled into a large, unused parking lot. The lot was empty; there were no other cars in it. There was grass growing from cracks in the lot. There were broken glass bottles and pieces of litter everywhere. A stray dog was walking around.

The parking lot was dark; there were no street lights. The driver stopped and removed his seat belt.

"Last stop," he said. He took another drink

and wiped his lips on his shirt sleeve. "Time for all pretty girls to get off my bus."

Amber stood up. He opened the bus door and pointed to it.

She shook her head. "This isn't my stop. What do you think you are doing?" "You will find out soon," he said. "Get off the bus." She took out her phone, but there was no time. He moved toward her fast.

Amber pressed the call button, but it dialled the last person she'd called--her sister!

"Hi, Sis," said Amber's sister, Aisha. "Do you know how late it is?" The driver knocked the phone out of Amber's hand.

"Help! I'm on a bus and the driver is crazy!"

The bus driver stomped on the phone with his boot. Amber could not get past him. He was holding up both arms. She could not exit the bus now.

I should have got out when I had the chance, she decided. But, every bus has an emergency exit!

She turned and ran to the back of the bus. The driver followed her. Amber made it to the emergency back door and turned the door handle. She kicked back at the driver, and he stopped for a second. He was out of breath. "Don't run away from me," he said. "I'm not a fast runner."

Opening the door, Amber jumped down. Her ankle twisted and she fell on her knees. The driver took a slow step down. It was hard for him to move around. He was in very bad physical condition, but he looked at her and smiled.

He was in no hurry now.

Vocabulary study

•**bother-***verb*- to annoy, worry or upset somebody; to cause somebody

•trouble or pain [e.g. The thing that bothers me is…]

•**caveman-** *noun-* a person who lived in a cave thousands of years ago; a man who behaves in an aggressive way.

•**grab-** *verb-* to take or hold something/somebody with your hand suddenly or roughly. [e.g. He grabbed hold of me and would not let go.]

•**scratch-** *verb-* to rub your skin with nails, usually because it is itching.

•**mysteriously-** *adverb-* in a way that is difficult to understand or explain; strangely. [e.g. Mystreiously, the streets were deserted.]

•**bloodshot-adjective-** [of eyes] with the part that is usually white full of red lines because of lack of sleep, etc.

•**professional-adjective-** doing something as a paid job rather than as a hobby.[e.g. She began her professional career as a teacher in 2022].

•**weird-adjective-** very strange or unusual and difficult to explain. [e.g. I had a really weird

dream last night.]
- **crack-verb-** to break without dividing into separate parts; to breaksomething in this way. [e.g. He cracked a bone in his arm.]
- **get off-verb**- to leave a train, bus or aircraft.

A. MATCH THE WORDS WITH THEIR SYNONYMS

Bother	A man from cave
Caveman	B. Seize
Grab	C. Claw
Scratch	D. trouble
Mysteriously	E. secretly
Bloodshot	F. Turned red
Professional	G. Leave
Weird	H. perfect
Crack	I. Break
.Get off	J. supernatural

1.   6.
2.   7.
3.   8.
4.   9.
5.   10.

B. *For each question, choose TRUE or FALSE*

options if the word in italics has been used correctly
1. Amber looked around at the empty seats on the bus. It was a large city bus.
   TRUE__ FALSE__
2. Her twin got on the bus after her.
   TRUE__ FALSE__
3. She was the first passenger on it. The city was asleep. It was almost two o'clock in the morning.
   TRUE__ FALSE__
4. The driver looks like a hairy caveman .
   TRUE__ FALSE__
5. When she got on the bus , it was nearly twelve, and the sun was shining. TRUE__ FALSE__
6. The bus driver stomped on the phone with his boot.
   TRUE__ FALSE__
7. Amber pressed the call button, but it dialled the last person she'd called--her sister!
   TRUE__ FALSE__
8. The driver was not professional that is why she was running.
   TRUE__ FALSE__

C. Read the story again and circle the most appropriate answer to the question.
1. Who was the last person she'd called?
a) The police
b) Her sister
c) Her mother
2. What were there?

a) broken glass bottles and pieces of litter everywhere.
b) The police officer
c) Her twin sister
3. What did she think what there was inside the bottle?
a) Poison
b) Water
c) It was not water
4. How well was the driver at driving the bus?
a) He was expert
b) He did not know how to drive
c) He was professional

5. Write a short review for the story

_____
_____
_____
_____
_____
_____
_____
_____
_____
_____

Chapter 2

Amber saw an old abandoned warehouse. The parking lot they were in was for the warehouse employees. But now, this business was gone. Closed forever. Most of the businesses in this part of town were closed. The buildings were not used by anyone. There weren't any houses around here either.

This was the emptiest part of town. Even if she screamed, no one would hear her.

"Why did you bring me out here?" she asked. She knew it was a dumb

question, but she wanted to keep him talking. Perhaps she could talk him out of his plan. She could make him realize he was making a mistake. She could tell him that he didn't want to hurt her.

"You need more patience," the hairy driver said, walking toward her. His walk was funny. He walked more like a duck than a person. But, there was nothing funny about his behaviour. "Have patience," he said again. "You're going to learn why I brought you here. I will teach you. I'm going to teach you until you understand."

"You're crazy!" she yelled, talking a step back. "Somebody help me!" "Love is crazy. And I'm in love with you!" He laughed again, then spit

something on the ground. "By the way, you can yell and scream as much as you

want to...but it won't do any good."

Amber turned in a circle, looking around her. She already knew he was right.

No one could save her. She was alone.

Then, she saw something. Amber saw a small light in the darkness. There was only one tiny light coming from a small old building. The building was on a side street back behind the warehouse. Inside, a golden light was flickering.

Is that a candle? she wondered, since the light was not steady. It was flickering like a candle flame. If there is a candle, then somebody must be inside! They would not leave a candle burning by itself.

She ran in the direction of the flickering light. Her ankle was hurting her, but she had no choice. She had to take the pain. The man behind her was coming. He was not going to change his mind.

"Young lady, there is no reason to run away," he said. "You'll like me once you get to know me better."

"That's not going to happen!" she shouted. "Get away from me!" "Where are you running to? There is nobody out here!"

She kept going even though her foot was hurting a lot. She was getting nearer to the building with the candlelight. It seemed like that was the only place to go.

It was hard to see. The night was darker than

usual. There were clouds in the sky covering the stars. The moon was hiding behind the clouds too. But, Amber could see on top of the building. On the roof of the building was a cross.

Is that a church? Out here in the middle of nowhere?

She got closer and saw, yes, it was a church. The church looked abandoned too. Some of the windows were broken. Wooden boards were falling off the sides. The grass around the area was very tall.

No one had come here in many years.

If no one uses it, why is there a candle burning inside? I hope it isn't a homeless person living in there.

But, she changed her mind. Even if it was a homeless person, perhaps they could help her. Anything was better than fighting the crazy bus driver alone!

The front door was unlocked. Amber ran inside the empty church. She saw the candle in the window. There were candles in each of the windows, but there was nobody around.

She closed the door.

Oh no, there isn't a lock on it!

The bus driver was coming. He was walking fast, but he could not run. He was not in good enough shape for running. He was out of breath.

"I told you, don't make me chase you!" he said, looking through the window. His face was sweaty. He looked like an animal.

"Stop! Stop it! My sister will call the police. You heard me call her!"

"Yeah, but she doesn't know where you are." "The police can track my phone."

The driver was holding her phone. He raised it. It was destroyed. "You should have held onto it better," he said, smiling his creepy smile. "Now stop running, little lady. You've got nowhere else to go." Amber stood a step back. The driver was standing outside looking in the window. The door didn't have a lock on it. She needed to put something in front of the door to block him. There were a few heavy benches. She took one of the benches and started to drag it towards the door, but it was too late, he was coming in!

"Help!" she cried again. Where was the preacher for this place? Someone had to be here because there were candles! They weren't burned down yet… Who had lit the candles?

She tried to keep the door closed, but he was too heavy. He was pushing and pushing, and finally, he got inside. Amber punched at him with her fist, but she missed.

"Whoa, take it easy!" he said. "I don't want to fight you."

"You tricked me," she said. "This church…you live here, don't you? This is your place!"

"Are you kidding?" the bus driver said. He

threw her phone over his shoulder. "I have a nice apartment. I would never live in a church. That is just weird."

"But you put the candles in here. It was a trick to get me to come inside." "You're wrong about that first part. I did not put the candles here, but you're

right about the second part. Yes, it was a trick…"

Then, Amber heard the sounds of the other person in the building. Somebody else is here!

The man walked out from behind a large curtain. He was very tall and skinny with long black hair. He wore an old black suit. At first, Amber thought maybe he was a preacher.

Like the bus driver, the man smelled terrible. He looked like he had not taken a shower in a long time, and he looked very hungry.

"Hi Fred," the fake preacher said to the bus driver. "Nice catch. You brought a good one tonight. But next time, bring me something to eat. You know I always like a good cheeseburger!"

"Stop complaining," the driver said. "And why did you call me Fred? Now she knows my name!"

"So? Who will she tell?"

Amber was trapped between them now. The driver was standing in front of the door, and the preacher was walking closer and closer.

"You're right," said Fred the bus driver. He

looked at Amber with his red eyes. "The dead tell no secrets."

Vocabulary study

- **warehouse-noun-** a building where large quantities of goods are stored, especially before they are sent to shops to be sold.
- **yell-verb**- to shout loudly, for example because you are angry, excited, frightened or in pain
- **scream-verb-** to give a loud high shout, because you are hurt, frightened ,excited, etc.
- **behavior-noun-** the way that somebody behaves, especially towards other people.
- **flame-noun-** a hot bright scream of burning gas that comes from something that is on fire.
- **Flicker- verb-** to keep going on and off as it shines or burns [e.g. The lights flickered and went out.
- **Abandoned-adjective-** left and no longer wanted, used or needed. [e.g. There was found abandoned but unharmed.]
- **Unlocked- adjective-** not locked
- **preacher-noun-** a person often a member of the clergy, who gives us religious talks and often performs religious ceremonies, e.g. in a church
- **trick-noun-** something that you to make somebody believe something that is not true, or to annoy as a joke.

A. MATCH THE WORDS WITH THEIR SYNONYMS

Warehouse	Flare
Yell	Cry out
Scream	Storehouse
Behavior	Left
Flame	Clergyman
Flicker	Shout
Abandoned	Unfastened
Unlocked	manner
Preacher	Joke
Trick	blaze

1.   6.
2.   7.
3.   8.
4.   9.
5.   10.

B. *For each question, choose TRUE or FALSE options if the word in italics has been used correctly*

1. Most of the businesses in this part of town were closed.
   TRUE__ FALSE__
2. He walked more like a duck than a person.

TRUE__ FALSE__
3. Amber saw a new castle on her way.
   TRUE__ FALSE__
4. There were a few heavy ladders. She took one of the ladders and started to drag it towards the door.
   TRUE__ FALSE__
5. She threw her phone over her shoulder.
   TRUE__ FALSE__
6. The man who walked out from behind a large curtain was very tall and skinny with long black hair. He wore an old black suit.
   TRUE__ FALSE__
7. At first, Amber thought maybe he was a preacher.
   TRUE__ FALSE__
8. The man smelled like a dirty toilet.
   TRUE__ FALSE__

C. Read the story again and circle the most appropriate answer to the question.

1. Before shooting him, where did she take the gun?
a) Under the bed
b) Out of her pocket
c) Out of her purse
2. Who was belong to these words: "Sometimes. A man needs a hobby, doesn't he?"
a) AMBER
b) FRED
c) STRANGER
3. How much money did she offer in order let go?
a) a thousand dollars
b) a million dollars

c) a thousand and five hundred dollars
4. How well was Amber at guns?
a) Not good
b) Bad
c) Expert

5. Write a short review for the story

_____
_____
_____
_____
_____
_____
_____
_____
_____
_____
_____

Chapter 3

Amber pleaded with the two men. "You don't have to do this," she said. "You can stop now. You can let me go!"

The fake preacher looked at his partner, Fred the bus driver. "You are very persuasive, young lady," he said. He smelled like a dirty toilet. He reached his hand into his pocket. Amber watched, wondering what he was going to do. He took out half of a cheese sandwich from his pocket and started eating it. "You think we should let you go?"

"Yes!"

"And you won't tell anybody?" "No, I swear!" she said.

"You won't tell anyone what we tried to do?"

"If you let me go, I won't tell," Amber said. "But--have you two done this to other people? Have you done this before?"

Fred laughed and coughed. "Sometimes. A man needs a hobby, doesn't he?" He wiped sweat from his beard and took a step closer. "Listen honey, you aren't going to talk your way out of this. We won't let you go. So relax." "Wait," the preacher said. "Let her finish talking. There is no rush. I like the sound of her voice."

"I like the sound of her screams," Fred said. "I don't care about the sound of her talking though."

Amber raised her hands. She was still holding her purse. "Guys, I want to give you every chance I can. I want you to realize that you have a choice. You can stop this at any time."

The preacher sat down on a bench. He crossed his legs and stared at her. He seemed very interested. "You want to give us 'every chance.' What do you mean? You have no power here. You are our prisoner."

"She just likes to talk," Fred said. "Tell her to be quiet. Let's get on with this!"

Amber ignored Fred. She sat down on the bench next to the preacher. "I'm saying, you two are adults. You have free choice. You can be criminals or you can act normal. You don't have to hurt people. You're right, I'm your prisoner. You're right, I have no power here. But, you do have power…the power to release me. Right now! And, you don't ever have to do this again."

"We like doing it," Fred said, crossing his arms. "And, if you don't shut up, I'm going to--"

"What? Kill me?" Amber asked. "I already know you're going to kill me.

So, I have nothing to lose. Do I?"

"Oh, you have something to lose," Fred said. "And, you are going to lose it very soon."

"Then let me buy my way out," she said, opening her purse. "I have a thousand dollars in here. I'll give it to you if you let me go."

The preacher shook his head. "The money is already ours. Everything you have is ours."

"Darren, would you please stop talking to her?" Fred said.

"Oh, you didn't want me to call you Fred," the preacher said, standing up, "but now, you're saying my name!"

"Because you were right!" Fred said, taking a big breath. "What difference does it make, Darren? Who is she going to tell?"

"You're both right," Amber said. "I won't tell anyone and you won't either."

She took her small gun out of her purse and shot Darren, the fake preacher once. Calmly, she stood up from the bench. She pointed the gun at Fred who raised his hands in the air. Amber kept her eyes on him, then she pointed the gun back at Darren and shot him two more times. She wanted to make sure he was dead.

"Whoa! Don't kill me!" Fred said. "We were just messing around. We weren't really going to hurt you!"

"You said you've done this before?"

"No, I… I was lying. It wasn't true. I only said that to scare you."

"I gave you every chance to let me go, didn't I? Over and over, I kept saying

you can stop," she said, pointing the gun at his stomach. "Things did not have to end like this. This didn't have to happen."

"I swear," Fred said, sweating again. He was trying to walk backward, but he hit a bench. "We weren't going to do anything to you. Our plan was to let you go."

"No it wasn't."

"It was! We weren't going to hurt you!"

"But I'm going to hurt you," she said, shooting him two times. Amber was an expert with guns. She knew exactly where to shoot someone if she wanted to kill them. She also knew where to shoot them, so they would not die.

Fred fell on the ground yelling and screaming. He was in pain, but he would not die, at least not for a few hours. Amber sat down and rested her injured foot.

"There is a little game I like to play with my sister," she explained. "We've been doing it for almost a year. We stay out late. We stay out until someone tries something stupid. Someone like you and the 'preacher' over there."

Her foot began to feel better, so she stood up. She picked up one of the burning candles.

"We let the stupid person or persons try to take us. Then, when they don't expect it, we kill them." She poured melted candle wax on Fred's beard. He yelled again.

"You tricked us!" he said.

"You tricked me first," she said. "I gave you the opportunity to stop. Do you want to give me the same chance? You want to give me a chance to stop?" She pointed the gun at his head. "I have one bullet left."

"Yes, yes! You can stop! You don't have to shoot me again!"

"Okay," she said, putting her gun back into her purse. "See? You convinced me. I won't shoot you again."

Amber held the candle to the man's pants. Fred's pants caught on fire. Then, she quickly ran out of the old church. She picked up her broken phone on the way out. Amber had another working phone in her bag, of course.

Aisha, Amber's twin sister, pulled her car up into the parking lot.

Right on time!

"Hi Sis," Aisha said, as Amber got into the car. "Looks like you won tonight."

The identical twin sisters sat in the car as the church caught fire.

"Thanks for playing 'Twin's Revenge,'" Amber said to the dead men in the church, smiling as her sister drove away.

Vocabulary study

• ***Plead with-verb*** - to ask somebody for something in avery strong and serious way. [e.g. I was forced to plead with him to go.]

• ***Persuasive-adjective*** - able to persuade somebody to do or believe something [e.g. There are several persuasive arguments in favour of the move.]

- ***Criminal-noun-** a person who commits a crime*
- ***Point-verb-*** to stretch out your finger or something held in your hands towards somebody or something in order to show somebody where a person or thing is.
- ***Backward-adjective-***directed or moving towards the back. [e.g. She strode past him without a backward glance.]
- ***Pour-verb*-** to make a liquid or other substance flow from a container in continuous stream, especially by holding the container at an angel.
- ***Bullet-noun-*** a small metal object that is fired froma gun
- ***Convince-verb-*** to make somebody believe that something is true
- ***Drive away-verb*-** to leave in a vehicle; to take somebody away in a vehicle
- ***Scream-verb*-** to shout

A. MATCH THE WORDS WITH THEIR SYNONYMS

Plead with	Not forward
Persuasive	Splash
Criminal	Ball
Point	Persuade

Backward	Give a lift
Pour	Beg
Bullet	Show
Convince	Convincing
Drive away	yell
.Scream	lawbreaker

1.   6.
2.   7.
3.   8.
4.   9.
5.   10.

B. *For each question, choose TRUE or FALSE options if the word in italics has been used correctly*
1. The preacher kept a sandwich in his pocket.
   TRUE__ FALSE__
2. The preacher likes Amber's screams.
   TRUE__ FALSE__
3. Amber kept talking because they were waiting on the police.
   TRUE__ FALSE__
4. Aisha know where to go because she had a second phone in her purse.
   TRUE__ FALSE__
5. The night darker was than usual, because the sky was cloudy.
   TRUE__ FALSE__

6. Amber could not stop the driver from coming into the church because she forgot to lock it.
TRUE__ FALSE__
7. The second man reminded Amber of the police.
TRUE__ FALSE__
8. The second man was very tired.
TRUE__ FALSE__

D. Read the story again and circle the most appropriate answer to the question.
1. How long have they been playing this game with her twin sister?
a) Almost a year
b) It was the first time
c) For five years
2. How many times was he shot?
a) Once
b) Twice
c) He was not shot
3. What did she pour on Fred's beard?
a) melted candle wax
b) a sandwich
c) melted wax
4. What was their game's name?
a) Revenge
b) Shooting
c) twin's revenge
6. **Write a short review for the story**

_____
_____
_____

Story-4
Persistence Pays
Chapter-1

"Why can't we come in?," I asked the large man standing in front of us. He was wearing a dark suit, and he was tall and strong. He was blocking the door to Zara's Nightclub. We could hear the loud dance music behind the door. We wanted to go in!

I had lost my job the other day. I needed to have a night of fun! I didn't want to have a lot of stress, so we had to find a way to get inside!

The tall man was a bouncer; his job was to let the "right" people in, and to keep everyone else out. He pointed to his clipboard and frowned. "Your name isn't on this list."

I looked up at him. He was at least six inches taller than me. "How do we get on that list?"

My friends--Nate and Aaron--and I had dressed up. We had driven across town to come to Zara's. The new club was famous and we wanted to check it out.

But, the bouncer did not reply. Instead, he looked over my skinny shoulder.

There was a long line of people behind me.

"How do I get in?" I asked again and I snapped my fingers. I was trying to get his attention.

"You don't," he said. He waved the next

guest in the line to come forward.

She was a beautiful blonde girl. When I saw her, I had an idea...

"Wait, wait!" I protested. "Our girlfriends are already inside!" It was a lie.

Aaron looked at me in a strange way. Perhaps he thought, "Is Jack crazy?"

"Jack, what are you doing?" Aaron yelled in my ear. He was a good-looking guy, but he was also shy. He never took any risks.

"Be quiet," I whispered back. I didn't want the bouncer to hear.

But, he did hear us. He rolled his eyes and tried to ignore me again. "No, really," I persisted. "Our girlfriends are inside, waiting for us." He lifted a red velvet rope to let the blonde girl pass.

"Thanks Bruce," she said as she walked by him. I could smell her perfume. I wanted to follow her in, but Bruce, the bouncer, shook his head at me.

"Are your friends really inside?" "Yes," I answered. "Our girlfriends!"

His expression was doubtful. He rubbed his bald head, then he lifted his clipboard again. "Okay. What are their names?"

"Their...names?" Well, I didn't know their names...because they didn't exist! "Uhh..."

"You're done," he said. He smiled and he pushed me aside. "Next!"

We could not get in, so we left Zara's. We

went across the street for coffee. "That was dumb, Jack," Aaron said, and he took off his jacket. He had put

on his favourite clothes to come out. With his good looks and clothes, he could be an actor, but his attitude was always negative.

I felt bad because it had been my idea to go out. Everyone knew it was impossible to get inside Zara's without a reservation…and reservations were impossible to get! But, I had wanted to try.

Nate ordered his coffee black, along with two chocolate-glazed donuts. Nate was very different from Aaron. He was more adventurous and happy. Nate loved to eat sweets like cakes and candies, so he was a bit overweight.

"I'll have the same," Aaron told the waiter. "But, unglazed donuts please." "And what would you like, sir?" the waiter asked me.

"I would like to know how to get into that nightclub," I told him.

"You can't get in there. Not without a reservation…or a date," he said. "Unless you are a female, of course. It is easy for the girls to go in. They want more girls inside."

"Why?" Aaron asked.

"Because the guys will go there and spend money!" I nodded. "That's unfair."

The waiter shrugged his shoulders. "Maybe, but that's life. If you want to go to Zara's, you will have to find someone to go with you. You want to order anything?"

"Just coffee with milk. No donuts." I looked at my friends. "Who eats donuts at nine o'clock at night?"

Nate and Aaron exchanged looks. "We do," they said together. I sighed and crossed my arms. It looked like I was going to be spending the evening with these two. *

After our coffees (and donuts) were finished, we paid our check. I noticed three girls sitting at a table. They were talking. They were also finished with their food and drinks.

"Guys, look," I said to my friends. "What if-_"

"No," Aaron said, cutting off my sentence. "Jack, let's just go." "Wait. What, Jack?" Nate asked. "Do you want to talk to them?"

I combed my black hair back with my fingers. "We can try. Why not? Come on, I just lost my job. Do me a favour! What is the worst thing that can happen?"

Aaron stared at me, but Nate punched him in the arm. "Come on, Aaron!" he said. "Jack is right. We can ask them. Perhaps they will want to go with us to Zara's. If we get inside, they can stay with us. Or, they can leave us if they want to."

The girls were watching us. One of them, a girl with red hair, leaned over the table. She whispered something to her friends and they nodded. None of them were smiling.

I felt a lump in my throat, but decided to go forward. I walked over to their table. My friends stayed behind me.

"Hi, my name is Jack Cruz. No relationship to Tom Cruise," I said, making a bad joke.

"Clearly," the redhead said. Her friends laughed, but I laughed with them. A little.

"Would you like to go to Zara's with us? The bouncer would not let us in," I said. "But maybe, we could get in with dates."

The smallest of the three girls said, "Dates? We don't even know you!" "I know," I said. "But let's just try! Don't you want to see inside Zara's?"

The girls looked through the window at the long line in front of the nightclub. Then they looked at each other.

"We don't need you to get inside," said the redhead. "But…I guess we can help you boys out. By the way, my name is Caprice."

Vocabulary study

•***Bouncer-noun***- a person employed to stand at the entrance to a club, pub, etc. to stop people who are not wanted from going in, and to throw out people who are causing trouble inside.

•***Clipboard-noun***-a small board with a clip at the top for holding papers, used by somebody who wants to write while standing or moving around.

- ***Snap-verb***- to break something with a sharp noise; to be broken in this way.
- ***Protest-verb-***to say or do something to show that you disagree with something or think it is bad, especially publicly.
- ***Doubtful-adjective-*** not sure, uncertain and feeling doubt
- ***Dumb-adjective-***stupid, ***verb***- to make something less accurate or educational, and of worse quality, by trying to make it easier for people to understand.
- ***Chocolate-glazed-adjective***- chocolate covered with glaze
- ***Donut-noun***- a small cake made of fried dough, usually in the shape of a ring, or round and filled with jam, fruit, cream and etc.
- ***Stare at-verb-*** look at somebody or something for a long time.
- ***Lump-noun***- a piece of something hard, solid, usually without a particular shape

A. MATCH THE WORDS WITH THEIR SYNONYMS

Bouncer	Doughnut
Clipboard	Look at
Snap	Club guard

Protest	A writing board
Doubtful	Break
Dumb	disagree
Chocolate-glazed	Hesitant
Donut	Speechless
Stare at	Piece
Lump	Chocolate with glaze

1.   6.
2.   7.
3.   8.
4.   9.
5.   10.

B. For each question, choose TRUE or FALSE options if the word in italics has been used correctly

1.   We could hear the loud dance music behind the door.
TRUE__ FALSE__
2.   He was a good-looking guy, but he was also shy. He always took any risks.
TRUE__ FALSE__
3.   The tall man wanted to be a bouncer; because to let the "right" people in, and to keep everyone else out was his favourite activity.
TRUE__ FALSE__
4.   He was at least six inches taller than me.

TRUE__ FALSE__
5.   Everyone knew it was possible to get inside Zara's without a reservation…and reservations were also possible to get!
TRUE__ FALSE__
6.   He lifted a red velvet rope to let the blonde girl leave.
TRUE__ FALSE__
7.   With his good looks and clothes, he could be an actor, but his attitude was always negative.
TRUE__ FALSE__
8.   Nate ordered his coffee black, along with two chocolate-glazed donuts.
TRUE__ FALSE__

C. Read the story again and circle the most appropriate answer to the question.
1. How was Aaron's character?
a) He was more adventurous and happy
b) He was so careful
c) He was not overweight
2. What did Nate love to eat?
a) Fruits and candies
b) sweets like cakes and candies
c) foods like sandwich
3. How many girls were there around the table?
a) Only one
b) No girls
c) Three girls
4. What were the girls doing before finishing with their food and drinks?

a) Talking
b) Drinking
c) Phoning

D. Write a short review for the story

_____
_____
_____
_____
_____
_____
_____

Chapter-2

"Let me talk to the bouncer," I said, as the six of us left the café. "No," Caprice said, "Let me. You couldn't talk your way in before."

I began to protest, but Nate nudged me in the ribs. "She's right. Give her a chance."

We started walking toward the back of the line. Caprice grabbed my hand suddenly. We ran toward the bouncer. The others followed us. They did not understand her plan.

"Excuse me, Bruce?" she shouted, waving her hand in the air. She stopped only inches away from the intimidating bouncer. "You're Bruce, aren't you?"

"Do I know you?"

"You were supposed to let my boyfriend in earlier," she said, pointing at me. "What happened?"

"His name wasn't on the list…"

"The list? Do you mean the fake list?" she asked, grabbing at his precious clipboard. He pulled it away from her and held it up, but she was persistent. "Get real! It's a bunch of fake names on a piece of paper."

"How do you know?" Bald Bruce asked, as he bent down to get closer to her. Perhaps he did not want the rest of the line to hear. "And, so what if it is fake?"

"Do you know a woman named Zara Bernhart?" Bruce stiffened. "The owner?"

"Yeah, the owner." Caprice reached into her handbag. It's a bunch of fake names on a piece of paper."

I'm Caprice Bernhart. Zara's my mom."

"That was awesome," I said, brushing my black hair out of my eyes. "I had no idea who you were!"

"Were?" Caprice said, leading me to the bar. "I still am! What are you having?"

Several customers were trying to get the helpless bartender's attention, but when he saw Caprice, he walked over to her. "Nice to see you!" he shouted over the music. "Can I get you something?"

"A Coke," she said, "and…" She looked at me. "Me, too."

"What?" the bartender asked. "Sorry, I couldn't hear you, man!" "I'll have a Coke too!" I yelled.

Caprice seemed surprised by my order. "Don't you drink alcohol?" "I'm underage," I said, smiling.

"I hope not," she said, "or we're both in trouble." The bartender brought over our sodas. We took them to a table in a vacant corner. "Your friends disappeared."

"I see one of them on the dance floor," I said, pointing to Nate. He was dancing with the smallest of the girls. "They seem to get along! Look, they are smiling."

"What about the other one?"

"Aaron? He's...gone!" I could not see Aaron anywhere. I took my phone out of my pocket because I wanted to check my messages. Perhaps he had sent me a text message. Yes, he had texted me! "Looks like he decided to go home."

"Hey, guys," said the third girl, as she walked over to our table. "What's up?"

"Where were you?" Caprice asked. "Did you scare Aaron away?"

"I guess so," she said. Then she looked at me. "By the way, what's your name again?"

"Jack," I said. "And I'm sorry, you are...?"

"I'm Susan. The other girl's Aisha. Anyways, your friend was weird!"

"He's not weird, he's shy," I said. "As The Smith's song goes, 'shyness is nice, and shyness can stop you...'"

"'...from doing all the things in life you'd like to!'" Susan finished. "I love that song!"

"Really? They are one of my favourite bands--"

"Hey, you scared away your boyfriend," Caprice said to her friend. "Leave my date alone!"

Susan smirked. She was unhappy. "Fine. I'm going to the bar," she said, "and I'm putting my drinks on your tab. You will have to pay for them later!" She walked away. She went to stand in the crowd in front of the busy bar.

I was happy to hear myself called a "date."

"Thanks again for helping us," I said. "It was a hard week for me. It was difficult because I lost my job this week."

"Oh, that's terrible! What was your job?" She looked uncomfortable.

Why did I tell her I'd lost my job? I thought.

"Actually," I said, pointing at the bar. "I did that. I was a bartender." She bit her lip. She was thinking of something. "So," she said at last, "Is Zara's everything you dreamed of?"

I lo It also had very loud audio speakers on the walls. A professional DJ was playing the best music, and the dance floor was packed. But, there were also plenty of seats for people to sit and talk.

"I love it," I said. "I would love to come here every week." "Is that a hint?"

"Yes," I said. "I mean, if you want to act like you are my date again. I would love to call you…if you give me your phone number."

Caprice grinned and put out her hand. I reached out to take it, but she stopped me. "No, give me your phone."

"Oh." I handed over my phone. She took it and added herself to my contacts list.

"So now you have it. Don't post it on the Internet. It's private." Immediately, I dialled her number. I watched her phone light up. "Now you have my number too," I said. "You can put mine on the Internet. I don't mind.

Nobody ever tries to call me."

"Your mother doesn't own a nightclub," she said. "Does she?"

"I don't think so," I said, laughing. "Listen, I really want you to know…I did not know who you were when I talked to you in the café."

"I believe you," she said. "I know you weren't just trying to use me." "Well, I was trying to use you," I admitted, "but I was very honest about it."

This time, she laughed and looked away. Maybe I need to shut up, I thought.

"I need to get going soon," she said. "I told my roommate I would be home before eleven."

"You should live for yourself, not for others," I said. "I read that on a card or something."

Caprice gave me a wide grin. "I agree one hundred percent! But, my roommate lost her keys to the apartment. Do you think she should wait outside while I stay here with you?"

I made an innocent face. "I don't mind if she waits."

"Typical male," she said, standing up. "You have my number."

"You have mine," I said, getting up with her. I wanted to walk her to the exit. "Let's see who calls the other first. We could place a bet."

For a moment, her face turned serious.

"Never bet against me or my family, Jack. We have a history of never losing."

Vocabulary study

• ***Nudge-verb*** - to push somebody gently, especially with your elbow, in order to grab their attention.[e.g. He nudged me and whispered, 'look who has just come in'.]

• ***Intimidate-verb-*** to frighten or threaten somebody so that they will do what you want. [e.g. They were accused of intimidating people into voting for them.]

• ***Bend down-verb-*** to lean or make something lean in a particular direction. [e. g. He bent and kissed her.]

• ***Bartender-noun*** - a person who works in a bar, serving drinks

• ***Underage-adjective-*** done by people who are too young by law

• ***Weird-adjective-*** very strange or unusual and difficult to understand. [e.g. She is a really weird girl.]

• ***Shyness-noun-*** the feeling of being nervous or embarrassed about meeting and speaking to other people. [e.g. After overcoming her shyness, she could express herself.]

• ***Smirk- verb-*** to smile in a silly or unpleasant way that shows that you are pleased with yourself, know something that other people do not know or etc.

- ***Bet-verb-*** to risk money on a race or an event by trying to predict the result.
- ***Grin-verb-*** to smile widely

A. MATCH THE WORDS WITH THEIR SYNONYMS

nudge	A. smile
intimidate	B. gamble
Bend down	C. Poke
Bartender	D. Frighten
Underage	E. Turn
Weird	F. Barman
Shyness	G. Not grown-up
Smirk	H. Peculiar
Bet	I. Crush
10. grin	J. timidity

1.   *6.*
2.   *7.*
3.   *8.*
4.   *9.*
5.   *10.*

B. *For each question, choose TRUE or FALSE options if the word in italics has been used correctly*

1. It's a bunch of fake names on a piece of paper.
   TRUE__ FALSE__
2. I took my phone out of my pocket because I wanted to check my messages.
   TRUE__ FALSE__
3. I was happy to call it called a "date."
   TRUE__ FALSE__
4. As The Smith's song goes, 'shyness is nice, and shyness can stop you…'"
   TRUE__ FALSE__
5. It was a hard week for me. It was difficult because I lost my wallet this week."
   TRUE__ FALSE__
6. A professional DJ was playing the best music.
   TRUE__ FALSE__
7. I lost her keys to the apartment. Do you think she should wait outside while I stay here with you?
   TRUE__ FALSE__
8. We have a history of losing one day.
   TRUE__ FALSE_

C. Read the story again and circle the most appropriate answer to the question.
1. What's on a piece of paper?
a) A letter
b) A present
c) a bunch of fake names
2. Whose song was it? 'shyness is nice, and shyness can stop you…'
a) The Smith's
b) Caprice

c) Younger person's
3. Why was it a hard week for her?
a) It was difficult because she lost her letter this week.
b) It was difficult because she lost her job this week."
c) It was difficult because she lost her purse this week."
4. Why was she happy ?
a) Because she was lucky
b) Because she heard herself called a "date."
c) Because she heard herself called a "lucky"

D. Write a short review for the story

_____
_____
_____
_____
_____
_____
_____
_____
_____
_____
_____
_____
_____
_____
_____

Chapter-3

I waited three days before calling her. It was a long three days. It was hard to wait.

"You lose," Caprice said when she answered the phone.

"We didn't bet, remember? I was wondering…what are you doing tonight?"

She paused. She did not say anything for a moment. "My parents are having a small party at home. Some business partners are coming to their house. They want to talk about the nightclub. They are curious how it is doing."

"Are you going to go?" I asked.

"Yes, because they want my opinion. They want the opinion of a younger person. Maybe you should come over too!"

I laughed about that. "No! You want me to meet your parents? And you want me to talk about my opinion of their club?"

Caprice didn't laugh with me. "Yes. I want you to come. Why not? I think you are a very honest person--"

"But, you do not know me!"

"Women have intuition about people, Jack. Can you meet me by eight?"

We met outside her apartment. We took her car to her parents' home. The home was a giant mansion. There were two stories and twenty rooms. I counted the windows.

"What are you doing?" she asked me. She drove her car up the large driveway.
"I'm counting the windows." "Why?"
"I don't know. I am trying to see where the restroom is."
That was a dumb thing to say, I decided. I'd never been to a rich person's house before. Now I was going to have dinner with rich strangers. The strangers were this girl's parents!
I had good reasons to be nervous.
"Don't be nervous," she said. She was getting out of the car. "Just be yourself."
"What does that mean? People always say that! 'Be yourself, be yourself.' Of course I will be myself!"
"Okay, never mind," she said. She closed the car door hard. "You are acting weird. Be somebody else."
"Sorry. This night is weird. I don't know what to say to your parents." She knocked on the door. A butler answered. A butler!
"Hi, Jeeves," she said.
You're butler is not named Jeeves! I wanted to say.
"Very funny, young lady. Come inside. And welcome, mister…?" "Hi, I'm Jack Cruz," I said. I held out my hand.
The butler shook my hand. He said his real name was Pete, not Jeeves. He took us to the large living room. There were a dozen people sitting on

sofas. Two of them stood up. They walked over to Caprice and me.

"Hi darling," said a beautiful lady. She looked like Caprice, but she was older. "Is this your new friend? Hi, I'm Zara."

"I'm Jack," I said, and I held out my hand again. She did not shake my hand. Instead, she gave me a big hug. A handsome man with grey hair was standing behind her.

"My wife likes hugs," he said. "But I'll shake your hand." His handshake was like Superman's. "Call me Ismael."

I remembered the joke about the butler's name. I thought he was making a joke too. "Ismael? You are funny! You cannot fool me again," I said.

"No, it isn't a joke," Caprice said. "My dad's name is Ismael."

Zara laughed out loud. "I like your friend, Caprice," she said. "Please sit down, Jack. Let's chat."

We talked for a few minutes in the living room. Then, we moved to the dining room. Dinner was a delicious chicken curry. After dinner, we started to talk about their nightclub business.

"What was your impression of the place?" Zara asked.

"My impression? Well, the first thing I saw was the bouncer. He was not rude, but I do not think his reservation list is real."

"You think the reservation list is fake? Why do

you think that?"

Caprice and I smiled at each other. "I told him it wasn't real," Caprice said. "Many people want to come to the club," Zara said. She was moving her pearl necklace around her shirt collar. "We have to be careful. We cannot let everyone inside. There isn't enough room for everyone."

"There is another reason," Caprice's father said. "Some people want to come, but not spend money. Other people come to spend money. It's a business. We want customers with money."

"What do you think about the inside?" Zara asked. "Did you like it?"

I remembered the poor bartender. He was trying to help too many customers.

I had been a bartender too. I knew it was a hard job.

"I liked the inside, but you need an extra bartender," I said. "Your guy needed help. He had too many customers. There was a very big crowd. I felt sorry for him."

"Do you know any bartenders? Do you know anyone who needs a job?" Caprice asked. Zara and Ismael waited for my answer.

"Hmmm, yes. I do know a bartender that needs a job," I said. "And he works cheap."

By the end of the week, I had a new job--at Zara's Nightclub! My girlfriend, Caprice, came to visit me often. I became friends with the other bartender, Dennis. I also became friends with

Bruce, the bouncer.

"I can't believe it. You are lucky, Jack," Aaron said one night. He was shaking his head.

"Lucky?" I asked. Aaron was sitting alone. He sat beside Nate and Nate's new girlfriend, Aisha. "You're wrong, my friend. Luck was not the reason. Luck had nothing to do with it. It was persistence. In this life, persistence is the only way to get anything."

"Luckily," Caprice said, holding my hand, "Jack has plenty of that!"

Vocabulary study

- ***Curious-adjective-*** having a strong desire to know about something [e.g. She is such a curious girl that she never stops asking questions.]
- ***Intuition-noun-*** the ability to know something by using your feelings rather than considering the facts.
- ***Giant-adjective-*** a very large strong person who is often cruel and stupid; a very large and powerful
- ***Mansion-noun-*** a large and impressive house
- ***Driveway-noun-*** a wide hard path or a private road that leads from street to a house. [e.g. There was a car parked on the driveway.]
- ***Butler-noun-*** the main male servant in a large house. [e.g. The butler announced that dinner was served.]
- ***Handshake-noun-*** an act of shaking somebody's hand wit your own, used especially to say hello or

goodbye or when you have made an agreement.
- **_Fool-verb-_** to trick somebody into believing something that is not true.
- **_Pearl-noun-_** a small hard shiny white ball that forms inside the shell of an oyster and is of great values as a jewel.
- **_Bartender-noun-_** a person who works in bars, pubs

A. MATCH THE WORDS WITH THEIR SYNONYMS

Curious	Instinct
Intuition	Eager to know
Giant	massive
Mansion	barman
Driveway	Necklace
Butler	Stately house
Handshake	Deceive
Fool	Road
Pearl	Shaking
10. bartender	main servant

1. *6.*
2. *7.*
3. *8.*
4. *9.*
5. *10.*

B. For each question, choose TRUE or FALSE options if the word in italics has been used correctly

1. Women have intuition about people, as jack said.
   TRUE__ FALSE__
2. Nate does not have a new girl.
   TRUE__ FALSE__
3. The home was a giant mansion.
   TRUE__ FALSE__
4. She did not have to wait before calling her.
   TRUE__ FALSE__
5. His handshake was like Ismail's.
   TRUE__ FALSE__
6. Dinner was a delicious Indian curry.
   TRUE__ FALSE__
7. The beautiful lady looked like Caprice, but she was older.
   TRUE__ FALSE__
8. The first thing she saw was the bouncer. He was not rude, but she does not think his reservation list is real.
   TRUE__ FALSE__

C. Read the story again and circle the most appropriate answer to the question.
1. As Jack said, what have women have got about people?
a) A strong desire
b) An intuition

c) A peculiar imagination
2. How long did she wait before calling her?
a) Several days
b) Three hours
c) Three days
3. How many people were there sitting on sofas?
a) Twelve people
b) Hundred people
c) No people
4. What was his handshake like ?
a) Boxers'
b) Actors'
c) Superman's

D. Write a short review for the story

_____
_____
_____
_____
_____
_____
_____
_____
_____
_____
_____
_____

Story-5
Discussions on Dating
Chapter-1

"I cannot go on a date with you," Dawn said on the phone. She was in northern California for the summer. College was over until next term. She was enjoying the long summer break, but she missed her friend, Dan. He had gone to Nevada to take college courses over the summer.

Dawn knew her friend liked her. He had liked her for a long time, but he had never had the courage to ask her out until now, over the phone.

"Yes, you can go on a date with me!" he said.

Dawn was twisting her long dark hair around her finger. She was lying on her bed in her bedroom. She was trying to think of an excuse to say. "My parents would kill me if I dated you!"

"Why?" Dan asked. He was in Nevada – several hours away by car. Dan was outside, sitting in a park. He had met Dawn's parents. He knew they did not like him.

He had a lot of tattoos and ear rings. His blonde hair was very spikey and his clothes were a little wild. Dawn's family was conservative. They didn't like "wild."

So, Dan knew the reason why. He didn't need her to answer his question.

Instead, he asked, "Do you have to tell your parents?"

"Of course, I have to tell them. I don't keep secrets…" "But, you are a grown woman."

"Look--you're a nice guy, Dan" Dawn said, but she didn't get to finish.

"I am!" Dan said, interrupting. "You're right, I really am a great guy. A terrific guy! Your parents would love me if they knew me better. They would adore me!"

"I'm sure they would like you eventually. Maybe not 'love' or 'adore.' But yes, sure, they would think you are boyfriend material."

"Or don't say anything to them. I'm sorry, Dawn, but you're being very old- fashioned…"

"What is wrong with that? I can't lie to my Mom and Dad," Dawn said, sitting up on her bed. "I won't."

"What, lying? Say nothing to them," Dan argued. He watched a woman jog by with her dog. "Don't tell them about me. That is not lying."

"Yes it is," she said. "It is a lie by omission."

"Oh, you are using the big words. 'Omission.' If you don't say anything, if you say nothing about me to them--"

"--then I have omitted the facts," Dawn said in a serious voice. But, she was only messing around. She was not really being very serious. "Anyways, omission is not a big word."

"I am failing my English class," Dan admitted. English was his second language. He was still learning. "So, it is a big word to me."

"If it is, then we're finished," she said, joking. "I cannot date someone with a small vocabulary."

"Ahh, but you would date me otherwise?"

Dawn laughed. "I guess you got me. Yes, I mean… I like you. There, I said it. Okay?"

"You said you like me," Dan replied. He had been sitting on a park bench.

Now he stood up. "Great. But, that does nothing for me." "What do you mean?" She had not expected him to say that.

"Think about it," he said. "Saying you like me makes it worse! Now I know you like me, so why can't we date? This is frustrating!"

"Let me finish," Dawn said. She got up from her bed. She was walking around the room. "I'm joking with you, Dan. I'll go out with you. When you are finished with your classes and you come back to California, we can see each other. But, I do have to tell my folks."

This was great news for Dan. His classes would be over next month, but he still wondered why she had to talk to her parents. It was very strange to him. "What do you need from them? You want to get their permission?"

"No, not their permission," she explained. "But it is our culture. You know, my family is not from America. We have different traditions where I am from."

"I know that. My family is the same."

"Yes, we came from another country. Where we come from, we respect our parents. We include our mothers and fathers in our daily lives."

"That isn't fair to say that. I respect my parents too!" "You do? Do you include them in your daily life, Dan?" "Well," Dan said, thinking. He did not really see them very often. He was away from home and did not go visit them very often. And, he did not ask their advice about things, but Dan did not want to tell Dawn any of that. "I try to call them every week," he said.

"That is not the same thing, but it does not matter. When will you be done with your summer term at college?"

"It is over next month. This is a very short term, you know. I am only taking these classes to make up for last term. I did not do well in class last term."

"Yes, I heard about that. You failed two classes," Dawn said. "But, I know you are very smart. You can do it!"

"Thanks," he said. "I do study a lot. In fact, my teachers know that I am a good student, but the classes are all in English. That is why I have trouble sometimes."

Dawn nodded. She understood completely. She had also had trouble last year in college, then she hired a professional tutor. The tutor helped her a lot. "When you come back, I'm going to help you study English," she said. "I will show you everything my tutor taught me."

"Really? That will help me a lot!" Dan said. "But, I need to do something first."

"What is that?"

"Before you can be my tutor," he said, smiling, "I will need to ask my parents."

"Very funny," Dawn said. "Just for that, I am going to be a very tough tutor!"

Vocabulary study

- ***Spikey-adjective-*** having sharp points
- ***Conservative-adjective-*** opposed to great or sudden social change; showing that you prefer traditional styles and values. [e.g. Her style of hair was never conservative.]
- ***Terrific-adjective-*** excellent, wonderful. [e.g. I feel absolutely terrific today.]
- ***Eventually-adverb-*** at the end of a period of time or a series of events. [e.g. Our flight eventually left five hours late.]
- ***Omission-noun*** - the act of not including somebody or something or not doing something; the fact of not being included or done.
- ***Frustrating-adjective-*** causing you to feel annoyed or impatient because you cannot do or achieve what you want. [e.g. It is frustrating to have to wait so long.]
- ***Matter-verb-*** to be important or have an

important effect on somebody or something [e.g. It does not matter to me.]
  • ***Trouble-noun-*** a problem, worry, difficulty, etc. or a situation causing this.
  • ***Completely-adverb-***in every way possible, finished
  • ***Tutor-noun-***a person who tarins person or a team.

A. MATCH THE WORDS WITH THEIR SYNONYMS

Spikey	Traditional
Conservative	Wonderful
Terrific	In the end
Eventually	Moving upwards
Omission	Exception
Frustrating	Annoying
Matter	coach
Trouble	Make important
Completely	Totally
Tutor	Worry

1.   6.
2.   7.
3.   8.
4.   9.
5.   10.

B. **For each question, choose TRUE or FALSE options if the word in italics has been used correctly**

1. She was in northern California for the summer.
   TRUE__ FALSE__
2. Dawn knew her friend liked her. He had liked her for a long time, also he had courage to talk over the phone.
   TRUE__ FALSE__
3. Although he had a lot of tattoos and ear rings ,His blonde hair was very spikey and his clothes were a little wild, Dawn's family was not conservative.
   TRUE__ FALSE__
4. Knowing that he likes her, but they cannot date is frustrating!
   TRUE__ FALSE__
5. The girl's problem was only permission.
   TRUE__ FALSE__
6. They came from another two countries.
   TRUE__ FALSE__
7. Dan did not use to see his parents very often.
   TRUE____ FALSE__
8. Dan used to take advice from his parents very often.
   TRUE__ FALSE__

C. **Read the story again and circle the most appropriate answer to the question.**

1. How far away from Dawn is Dan, if driving a car?
a) Twenty-four hours away
b) One day away
c) Several hours away

2. What reason did Dan give for failing two classes?
a) The classes were in English
b) The classes were in German
c) The classes were science and technology

3. Why did Dawn insist on telling her parents about Dan?
a) She was not allowed to date yet
b) She wanted them to give her money
c) She liked to include them in her life

4. Dan thinks her parents did not like him. Why?
a) Because they were a different religion
b) Because they had different ethnic backgrounds
c) Because they were conservative and he looks too wild

D. Write a short review for the story

_____
_____
_____
_____
_____
_____
_____

Chapter-2

Caprice loved talking on the telephone. She enjoyed chatting with her friends... especially about their boyfriends! It was a rainy day outside, and she was bored. She decided to call her old friend Dawn. She had heard a rumor and wanted to learn the truth.

"So, Dawn," she said, "Did you know Jack is in Nevada now?"

"Really?" Dawn said. "I remember your boyfriend Jack! He's cute. Very handsome. What's he doing out there in Nevada?"

"He's talking summer classes. In fact, you'll never guess where."

"You're right," Dawn said. She hated guessing games. Besides, she was in a hurry. It was almost time to start work. She was putting her clothes out on the bed. She was not really paying attention. "Nevada is a big state. I do not know where Jack could be."

"Jack is at the same college as Dan!"

"Oh. That's interesting," Dawn said. She was not sure why Caprice was telling her this. "I'm sure Jack and Dan will be glad to hang out together. Do they know each other very well?"

Caprice smiled. "They know each other a little. They are becoming friends. In fact, they have been talking a lot lately. So, Dawn... Dan told Jack that you two are dating!"

Oh, so that's what this call is about, Dawn thought.

"Well... I would not say we are dating. But, I told him we could date. When he returns to California."

"Come on, don't be shy. I'm your friend. Tell me everything. You know, I used to date Dan. We dated two years ago when we were freshmen in college."

"I remember that," Dawn said. She remembered, but not very well. Caprice dated a lot.

"So, did you think you could keep this a secret from me?"

Dawn was getting ready for work. She looked at her clock. There were only twenty minutes to get dressed and get to her job. She did not have a lot of time to talk. "There isn't much to tell, Caprice. And, I'm in a little bit of a hurry."

"Just give me the main details then."

"Okay, fine. You are very persistent! Dan asked me to date him, but he didn't ask when he was here. He waited until he had gone to Nevada!"

"Men. They have very bad timing, don't they? I remember Dan was always late for things."

Dawn wanted to switch the subject. She did not want to think about Dan and Caprice as a couple. "What about you and Jack? Jack is so nice! You guys were seeing each other a long time. Are you two still a couple?"

"Not really," Caprice said. She had not told anyone this before. "Actually, we broke up before he left for Nevada."

"Oh, I didn't know that! You never told me. I'm sorry. So, you do not see him anymore?"

"We broke up on good terms. We are still friends. But--how can I say this?

Jack was not a good boyfriend."

Dawn knew her friend was very picky about her boyfriends. That is why there had been so many of them. Caprice usually only dated a person a few times, but she had stayed with Jack for a few months. Everyone thought they were a nice couple. In fact, Dawn thought Jack might even be the big one!

She was shocked to hear anything negative about Jack. "Not a good boyfriend? Why? What did he do?" She checked her clock again. She was running out of time, but she wanted to hear this, so she put the phone on speakerphone. She was able to dress while talking and listening.

Caprice said, "For starters--Jack likes to flirt with other women." "Oh, no. Are you serious? Was he… was he cheating on you?"

"I don't think so. No. I am sure he was not seeing anyone else, but I do not like my boyfriends to even look at someone else."

Dawn shrugged her shoulders. "Boys will be boys. Looking isn't touching. I mean, looking does not mean anything. You never looked at somebody else?"

"Maybe I did, but Jack was not just looking, he was talking to them too. He was flirting with them." "Where?"

"What?"

"Where was he talking to other women?" Dawn asked. "At the nightclub." "Where he works?"

"Yes. He still works at Zara's, my mom's nightclub. He is a bartender. He serves drinks to pretty girls all night long."

Dawn laughed, then covered her mouth.

"What's so funny?" Caprice asked. She was getting a little angry. "Sorry. Didn't you help him get that job?"

Caprice did not like to be reminded about that. "Yeah. I did help him get the job. If I could go back in time, I would stop myself."

"Well Caprice, be fair. If Jack is a bartender, then it is his job to talk to customers."

"I guess so."

"You guess so? Come on, be reasonable! You are not being fair. I mean, if he is talking to people at the club…"

"He's flirting with them. He is not just talking. There is a big difference!

Don't be naïve."

"I'm not naïve. You're being too picky. Maybe he is only speaking that way for tips. You know, he gets more money if he is extra nice. There is no reason to be jealous. He is only talking to be nice."

"He does not have to be that nice. Besides, you would not like it if Dan was acting that way. You would be jealous, wouldn't you?"

"No. Maybe I would not care. Right now, it does not matter. I am not yet dating Dan."

"Hmmm. That's true. You are single. So, if you are going to take Jack's side, then you date him! And, I'll take Dan!"

"What? Are you crazy?" Dawn asked. She did not have any time left. "Look, I have to go to work. I know you are joking, but that isn't funny."

"You said you do not get jealous. What's the problem?" Caprice asked.

Dawn sighed. She grabbed something to eat from her kitchen. She was going to have to eat at work. "We can have this conversation later. I do not have time to argue." She hung up the phone without saying goodbye to her friend.

Vocabulary study

•***Handsome-adjective-*** [of men] attractive, good-looking

•***Hang out-verb-***spend a lot of time in a

place.

• ***Persistent-adjective-***determined to do something despite difficulties , especially when other people are against you and think that you are being annoying or unreasonable

• ***Couple-noun-*** two people or things

• ***Picky-adjective-***(of a person) liking only particular things and difficult to please.

• ***Cheat-verb-*** to trick somebody or make them believe something that is not true.

• ***Shrug-verb-*** to raise your shoulders and then drop them to show that you do not know or care about something.

• ***Touching-adjective-*** causing feelings of sympathy; making you feel sad or emotional.

• ***Reasonable-adjective-*** fair, practical, and sensible

• ***Naïve-adjective-***not having enough knowledge, good judgement or experience of life and too willing to believe that people always tell you the truth.

• ***Jealous-adjective-***feeling angry or unhappy because somebody you like or love is showing interest in somebody else.

• ***Grab-verb-*** to take or hold somebody or something with your hand suddenly or roughly.

A. *MATCH THE WORDS WITH THEIR SYNONYMS*

Handsome	Deceive
Hang out	Have fun
Persistent	Gorgeous
Couple	Raise shoulders
Picky	Logical
Cheat	Purposeful
Shrug	emotional
Touching	Pair
Reasonable	Hold
.Grab	fussy

1. 6.
2. 7.
3. 8.
4. 9.
5. 10.

B. For each question, choose TRUE or FALSE options if the word in italics has been used correctly

1. Caprice loved talking on the telephone. She enjoyed chatting with her friends.
   TRUE__ FALSE__
2. She loved talking especially with her best friends.
   TRUE__ FALSE__
3. Dawn really loves guessing.

TRUE__ FALSE__
4. ... Dan told Jack that they were dating!"
   TRUE__ FALSE__
5. They dated many years ago when we were freshmen in the university. TRUE__ FALSE__
6. Dan was always late for things.
   TRUE__ FALSE__
7. They broke up before he left for Nevada.
   TRUE__ FALSE__
8. As knowing a lot about his boyfriend, She was not shocked to hear anything negative about Jack.
   TRUE__ FALSE__

C. Read the story again and circle the most appropriate answer to the question.

1. Why was Caprice bored?
a) Because the electricity went off
b) Because she did not have to work
c) Because it was raining outside
2. Who told Caprice that Dan asked Dawn on a date?
a) Zara
b) Dan
c) None of the above
3. Why did Caprice date a lot?
a) Because she was picky
b) Because she enjoyed dating different people
c) Because she was looking for a husband
4. Why did Dawn think Caprice was a jealous person?

a) Because Caprice thought all men cheat
b) Because Caprice thought Jack was cheating
c) Because Caprice thought Jack was flirting

D. Write a short review for the story

Chapter-3

Dan was very excited. His summer college courses were almost over. He was doing well in the courses. He would get good grades.

Good grades will help my grade point average, he thought. When I go back to my university in California, maybe I will get a scholarship.

He was glad to be leaving Nevada soon. In two weeks, he would be home. He could see Dawn again. She had promised to go on a date with him when he returned.

They had known each other a long time, but he had never had the courage to ask her out. It had been easier to ask over the phone. It was easier to ask when he was not there.

In some ways, it did not seem real. Dating Dawn had been his dream...

Soon, that dream is going to come true!

His phone rang. It was his friend Jack. He had known Jack for a long time, but they had never been close friends. Now, they were going to the same summer school. Now, they were becoming good friends. Sometimes, they ate lunch together. At night, they liked to watch movies together, when their studies were over.

But, Dan had always noticed that Jack was a little sad. Something was always bothering Jack. And now, Dan knew what it was...

"Hi, Jack," he said, answering the phone. "Dan! Hey, I need to talk to you."

"That's funny. I wanted to talk to you too."

"Oh," Jack said, a little surprised. "Alright, you can go first. What's going on?"

"Dawn told me you are not seeing Caprice anymore."

Jack was surprised again. He and Caprice had not made their break up public. "That's true," Jack admitted. "I didn't want to say anything. I was hoping Caprice and I would get back together."

"That is what I wanted to talk about," Dan said. "I could tell something has been bothering you, but I did not know what. I was worried about you."

"Thanks, man. I'm okay though. Really."

"Are you sure?" Dan asked. "Do you want to talk about what happened?" "Oh, you know how women are," Jack said. He laughed, even though he did not think it was funny. He was still friends with Caprice, but his feelings were very hurt. He did not think she had been fair to him. "She thought I was flirting with other women. She accused me of trying to attract a new girlfriend."

"Really? I have not known you very long," Dan said. "I mean, I did not know you very well, but I do now. You are a nice guy. That does not sound like you!"

"It isn't," Jack agreed. It felt good to have

someone to talk to. "I never did that! But, Caprice thinks I did. I cannot change her mind. She thinks I flirted with my customers."

"But you didn't?"

"I did a little, but it was not really flirting, just being extra nice. You know what I mean? It was totally innocent."

Dan asked, "What do you mean?"

"I only did it to get bigger tips," Jack said. "That is how those types of jobs work. You don't get paid very much, so you have to work for tips!"

Dan nodded. "I understand. I worked as a waiter in a restaurant. My salary was very low, but I was friendly. The customers loved me, so I made better tips than the others."

"Yes, that is exactly right!" Jack said. "It is simple. Why can't Caprice understand that? Hey, maybe you could talk to her."

Dan thought about that. "I don't think that is a good idea, Jack." "Why not?"

"I have to tell you something. It is not a big deal, but you should know. I dated Caprice for a little while; not very long, and it was a long time ago."

"Yes, I know," Jack said. "So what?"

"Well… Caprice is awesome," Dan said. "She is great. I will be honest, I liked her a lot back then, but actually, she was jealous of me too."

"What? She thought you were flirting with others?" Jack couldn't believe it.

He was not the first guy to deal with this problem.

"That's right. It sounds like you are having the same issue I had."

Jack was glad to be able to talk about these things. It was a relief. He had been quiet about his feelings… but now, he talked! But, Jack had forgotten--he wanted to ask Dan something too!

"Dan, I have a question. I started talking about my problems, and I forgot to ask you."

"That's okay. What's up?"

"It's about Dawn. You mentioned you were going to start dating her?"

"Yes. I have wanted to go out with her for a long time, but I was always too shy. I never asked her out, but finally, I did!"

"And she said yes?"

Dan paused. Why was he asking about Dawn suddenly? "Yes. She wanted to talk to her parents first. That's what she said. But--"

"Why does she want to do that?"

"I don't know. She said she likes to keep them involved in her life." "Doesn't that sound strange to you?"

"No. Maybe a little bit. Why are you asking this, Jack?" "I was just curious," Jack said. "Because she's…" "She's what?"

"You know she comes to Zara's sometimes.

The bar I work at?"

Dan didn't know that, but it did not matter to him. Lots of people go to the nightclub. "Why do I need to know about that?"

"Because she is one of my customers. I need to tell you something, Dan. I think Dawn is very cute. Sometimes, I talk to her when she comes to the club. I was thinking about asking her on a date."

"What?" Dan asked. He couldn't believe it! "Are you serious?"

"Listen to me. I'm not going to do it. I won't ask her out since she said yes to you, but I wanted to make sure. I don't have a girlfriend. Caprice broke up with me, so you know… I thought about Dawn."

"Sorry, man. I got to her before you did! You will have to work things out with Caprice!"

Vocabulary study

•*Courage-noun-*the ability to do something dangerous, or to face pain or opposition without showing fear.

•*Surprised-adjective-* feeling or showing surprise

•*Public-adjective-* connected with ordinary people in society in general. [e.g. The campaign is designed to increase public awareness of the issues.

•*Bother-verb-* to annoy, worry, or upset

somebody, to cause somebody trouble or pain. [e.g. That sprained ankle is still bothering her.]

•***Flirt-verb-*** to behave towards somebody as if you find them sexually attractive, without seriously wanting to have a relationship with them.

•***Accuse-verb-*** to say that somebody has done something wrong or is guilty of something

•***Innocent-adjective-*** not guilty, of a crime, etc. not having done something wrong.

•***Awesome-adjective-***very impressive or very difficult and perhaps rather frightening.

•***Mention-verb-*** to write or speak about something or somebody, especially without giving much information.

•***Curious-adjective-*** very interested in doing ang knowing something

A. MATCH THE WORDS WITH THEIR SYNONYMS

Courage	Lead on
Surprised	Charge
public	guiltless
bother	great
Flirt	cite
Accuse	bravery
innocent	trouble

awesome	Astonished
Mention	Interested
Curious	Related to government

1.　　　　　　6.
2.　　　　　　7.
3.　　　　　　8.
4.　　　　　　9.
5.　　　　　　10.

B. For each question, choose TRUE or FALSE options if the word in italics has been used correctly

1. *As* doing well in the courses, He would get good grades.
   TRUE____ *FALSE*__
2. He was frustrated to be leaving Nevada soon.
   TRUE__ FALSE__
3. He had promised to go on a date with her when he returned.
   TRUE__ FALSE__
4. She accused him of trying to attract a new girlfriend.
   TRUE__ FALSE__
5. Dan worked as a waiter in a restaurant. Salary was very low.
   TRUE__ FALSE__
6. Dawn and Dan have gone out many times before he left for Nevada.

TRUE___ FALSE___
7. Dan said that he likes to keep his parents involved in his life.
TRUE___ FALSE___
8. The bar Jack worked at was Zara's.
TRUE___ FALSE___

C. Read the story again and circle the most appropriate answer to the question.
1. Why was Dan in need of good grades?
a) He wanted a college scholarship
b) His parents were angry
c) The college was going to ask him to leave
2. What had Dan noticed about Jack?
a) That Jack seemed sad
b) That Jack liked to flirt
c) That Jack got good grades
3. Why did Jack say he was extra nice to customers?
a) Because he wanted tips
b) Because he wanted to date them
c) Because he was a very friendly person
4. Why did Dan understand Jack's reason for being extra nice to customers?
a) Because Dan watched Jack at work
b) Because Dan was Jack's friend
c) Because Dan worked as a waiter and also got tips

D. Write a short review for the story
_____

Answers

Story-1
The gift of the Magi
Chapter-1

1. e
2. d
3. j
4. h
5. f
6. i
7. g
8. a
9. c
10. b

1. false
2. false
3. true
4. true
5. false
6. true
7. false
8. true

1. a
2. b
3. c
4. a

Chapter-2

1. c
2. d
3. f
4. i
6. a
7. e
8. j
9. h

5.g   10.b

1.true   5.true
2.false   6.true
3.false   7.false
4.true   8.false

1.a
2.b
3.c
4.c
5.a

Story-2
SERMONS IN STONES AT BLOOMSBURY. THE NEW SCULPTURE ROOM AT THE BRITISH MUSEUM
Chapter-1
1.e   6.d
2.g   7.f
3.j   8.h
4.b   9.i
5.c   10.a

1.true   5.true
2.false   6.false
3.true   7.true
4.false

1.a
2.a
3.b
4.c

Story-3
The church

Chapter-1

A) 1.d   6.f
2.a   7.h
3.b   8.j
4.c   9.i
5.e   10g.

B) 1.true   5.false
2.false   6.true
3.false   7.true
4.true   8.false

C) 1.b
2.a
3.c
4.c

Chapter-2

A) 1.c   6.a
2.b   7.d
3.f   8.g
4.h   9.e
5.j   10.i

B) 1.true   5.false
2.false   6.true
3.false   7.true
4.false   8.true

C) 1.c
2.b
3.a
4.c

Chapter-3
A) 1.f   6.b
2.h   7.c
3.j   8.d
4.g   9.e
5.a   10.i

B) 1.true   5.true
2.false   6.false
3.false   7.false
4.true   8.true

C) 1.a

2.b
3.a
4.c

Story-4
Persistence pays

Chapter-1

A) 1.c   6.h
2.d   7.j
3.e   8.a
4.f   9.b
5.g   10.i

B) 1.true   5.false
2.false   6.false
3.false   7.true
4.true   8.true

C) 1.a
2.b
3.c
4.a

Chapter-2

A) 1.c   6.h
2.d   7.j

3.e   8.a
4.f   9.b
5.g   10.i

B)1.true   5.false
2.true   6.true
3.false   7.false
4.true   8.false

C)1.c
2.a
3.b
4.b

Chapter-3
A)1.b   6.j
2.a   7.i
3.c   8.g
4.f   9.e
5.h   10.d

B)1.true   5.false
2.false   6.false
3.true   7.true
4.false   8.true

C)1.b
2.c
3.a
4.c

Story-5
Discussion on Dating

Chapter-1

A) 1.d   6.f
2.a   7.h
3.b   8.j
4.c   9.i
5.e   10g.

B) 1.true   5.false
2.false   6.true
3.false   7.true
4.true   8.false

C) 1.b
2.a
3.c
4.c

Chapter-2

A) 1.c   6.a
2.b   7.d
3.f   8.g
4.h   9.e
5.j   10.i

B) 1. true   5. false
2. false   6. true
3. false   7. true
4. false   8. true

C) 1. c
2. b
3. a
4. c

Chapter-3
A) 1. f   6. b
2. h   7. c
3. j   8. d
4. g   9. e
5. a   10. i

B) 1. true   5. true
2. false   6. false
3. false   7. false
4. true   8. true

C) 1. a
2. b
3. a
4. c

Thank you for reading!

Congratulations on finishing it. I hope you have enjoyed these stories, and your English has improved as a result! A book is a source of widening our imagination and circle of thinking. A person who has a habit of reading a book every day will have benefits not only for our society, not only for themselves, will reach their objectives and will put a brick to their future. Bright and happy future is waiting for them. Never stop reading and learning.

-Kamolova Saida Zufar qizi

"Today a reader, tomorrow a leader." – Margaret Fuller

www.ingramcontent.com/pod-product-compliance
Lightning Source LLC
LaVergne TN
LVHW020447070526
838199LV00063B/4867